RACE CAR LEGENDS

The Allisons

Mario Andretti

Crashes & Collisions

Drag Racing

Dale Earnhardt

Formula One Racing

A.J. Foyt

Jeff Gordon

Motorcycles

Richard Petty

The Unsers

Women in Racing

CHELSEA HOUSE PUBLISHERS

RACE CAR LEGENDS

DRAG RACING

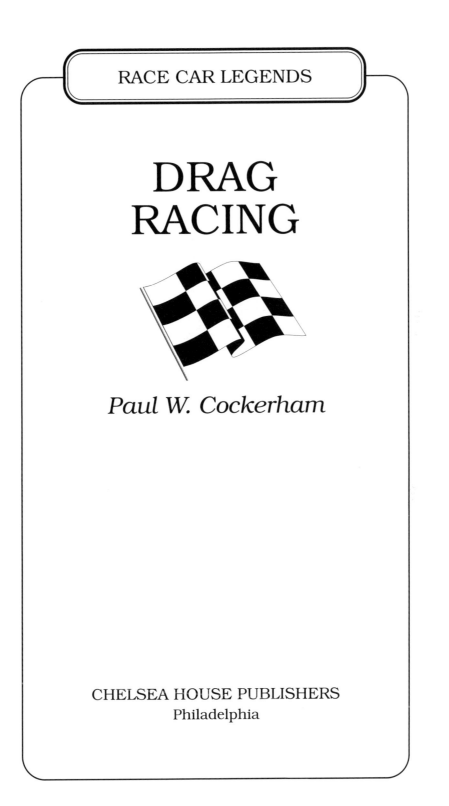

Paul W. Cockerham

CHELSEA HOUSE PUBLISHERS
Philadelphia

Produced by Daniel Bial and Associates
New York, New York

Picture research by Alan Gottlieb
Cover design by Takeshi Takahashi
Cover photo credit: ©1990 Jere Alhadeff

Frontispiece photo: Shelly Anderson

Many of the names and descriptions used in this text are the property of
various manufacturers and businesses. They are used here for identification
purposes only.

First Printing

1 3 5 7 9 8 6 4 2

ISBN 0-7910-4434-3

CONTENTS

A COOL
SPORT

L et's face it—drag racing is very cool. Even when seen on the TV, its sights and sounds make a big impression.

The cars are colorful, long, low, and lean. The engines crank out thousands of horsepower, flame and fury belching out from the exhausts with a roar that can leave you deaf. Fat rear tires launch the racers off the line, spinning wildly in huge clouds of smoke.

Drag racing is simple. The person who wins is the guy or gal who can cover a quarter mile—1,320 feet—the fastest. The best drivers and cars today can do so in under five seconds, at speeds greater than 300 miles per hour (m.p.h.). At this speed, special parachutes are used to bring the machines to a stop at the end of a run.

Drag racers need bravery and discipline to per-

Back when drag racing was just a contest between two drivers to see whose car was faster, a favorite site for racing was the paved bed of the Los Angeles River. In this photo from the 1950s, the police disperse racers near the Fourth Street Bridge.

form at their best. It takes a lot of concentration and hair-trigger reflexes to get a car off the line first, and skill and strength to keep these mechanical monsters under control as they roar down the quarter mile.

Organized drag races have been around for nearly 50 years, although stop-light challenges have no doubt been fought between drivers ever since cars were invented. Today, the sport is a celebration of the wonders of technology.

That technology starts with the drag strip itself. Covering such a short distance at such speeds means that it is often impossible for the naked eye to determine who a winner might be, so special computerized timing equipment, triggered by an infrared beam aimed at each car's front wheels, is used to measure driver reaction time, total elapsed time (ET) for a run, top speed (measured over the final 66 feet), and victory margin. The difference in ETs can be calculated to as little as one-ten-thousandth (.0001) of a second.

The fastest cars in drag racing, those that compete in the Top Fuel class, had eclipsed both the five-second ET mark and the 300 m.p.h. speed barrier by the start of the 1990s. In comparison, the quickest street cars, fresh from the dealer, are hard-pressed to cover the quarter mile in 12 seconds, or to reach a speed of 120 m.p.h. at the distance.

Drag racing has certainly come a long way. Historians of the sport agree that drag racing had its roots in the illegal street challenges that took place in southern California after the close of World War II. Now the sport, under the guidance of the National Hot Rod Association [NHRA] and other organizations, features a national tour that covers 18 events each year, drawing more than two million spectators annually to tailor-made facilities all across the United States (the sport is a favorite in Australia and in Europe as well). Prize money for the top three professional classes—Top Fuel, Funny Car, and Pro Stock—now totals in the millions of dollars.

A favorite "hot rod" from drag racing's earliest days would be a Ford roadster from the early 1930s (a 1932 "deuce" was a particular favorite) that had its fenders removed, the top lowered ("chopped") or removed, and a "flathead" V-8 engine modified with special camshafts, carburetors, cylinder heads, and exhaust systems. Today's top machinery is never driven on the streets and boasts high-tech touches such as onboard computers that monitor engine performance during a race.

Such a car can cost nearly $200,000. Professional race teams work out of full-size tractor-trailer rigs—basically fully-equipped rolling shops—that can cost another quarter-million dollars. The cars are tended by teams of specialized mechanics, led by a crew chief, and all are highly paid for their skills. Such teams are funded by corporate sponsors who pay as much as $2 million a year to have the names of their products painted on the sides of the race car.

It's a lot of money, but don't think that the corporate sponsors are crazy for spending it. By sponsoring a top team, they ensure that their product is seen by the 100 million or so people who see drag racing events on TV each year.

Racing at the top national events is done on the elimination system. Entrants first race the clock in qualifying runs, and then the top 16 qualifiers in each class go head-to-head. Losers pack up and go home, while the winners prepare themselves for the next round.

TOP FUEL DRAGSTERS

When you see a top fuel dragster for the first time, there is no mistaking the purpose for which it was built. They make the biggest impression when viewed from the rear, which is where all that horsepower makes contact with the pavement.

Standing several feet in the air at the very tail of today's top fueler is a huge rear wing. On an airplane, the shape of the wing creates lift, allowing the aircraft to fly. On a dragster, the wing is inverted, so that the air currents that pass it during a run put pressure on the rear wheels, increasing traction and speed.

Then there are the huge rear wheels, with their fat, slick, racing tires. The "slicks"—standard equipment for all classes of dragsters—are so named because they have no tread, which would decrease traction. They are run with very little air pressure. This causes the sides of the tires to appear wrinkled when the car is standing still, yet allows their circumference to grow when the driver stands on the gas, making the dragster that much faster.

The engine, out in the open, catches the eye next. A variety of suppliers make these aluminum V-8 engines, which are based on a Chrysler design called the "Hemi" (slang for the hemispherical shape of its combustion chamber) that was used in passenger cars up until the early 1970s. At 500 cubic inches, these engines are about twice the size of those used

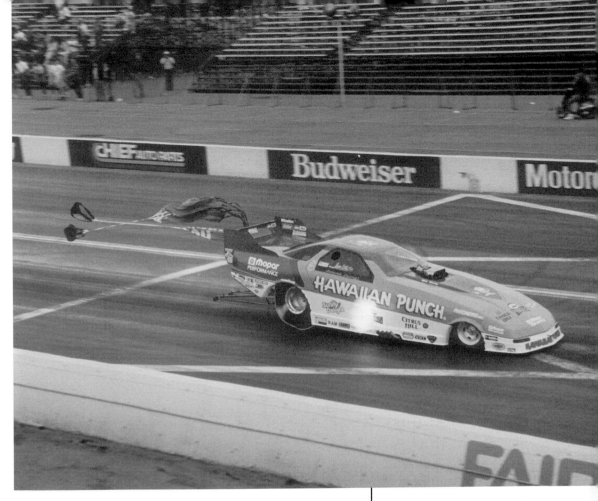

in today's passenger cars. The engines use fuel injection and are topped with superchargers, distinctive block-shaped units that compress the air that is mixed with the fuel in the engine's combustion chamber.

"Fuel," in the language of drag racers, means nitromethane, or "nitro" for short. It is highly combustible and produces far more horsepower than does the gasoline you get at the pump. (Other classes of dragsters do run on gasoline or alcohol.) And when a driver stands on the accelerator, nitro produces an ear-splitting, earth-shaking roar that race fans love, even though it means that those watching from the grandstands have to wear earplugs.

Just like top fuelers, funny cars use parachutes to slow the car down after it crosses the finish line.

A large crowd came out to see the first event sanctioned by the National Hot Rod Association in April 1953. Paul Wallace drops the green flag to start the race.

A stubby cylinder on the rear of the engine houses a multiple-plate clutch that top fuelers (and funny cars) use to transfer power from the engine to the drive wheels, instead of a transmission. Drag racers have learned over the years that transmissions and simpler clutch designs could not cope with the brute forces created by monster engines. Many such units blew up like grenades; several drivers lost their lives in such accidents or were maimed by metal fragments when clutches exploded.

One such driver was Don Garlits, who lost part of his right foot when his transmission blew up during a March 1970 run. Garlits was driving a front-engined "slingshot" top fueler, the standard design for the time, which placed the transmission right between the driver's feet. While "Big Daddy" was recovering from his injuries, he finalized his idea for a safer, rear-engine design, and is today credited with being the inventor of the rear-engine top fueler. (Garlits and his amazing career are featured in the next chapter.)

Thus the driver's compartment, and its protective cage of steel tubing, is found directly in front of the engine. Thin steel rails, covered with a magnesium skin, stretch to form the needle nose of the top fueler. Their length, which can mean a wheelbase of nearly 300 inches, helps keep the nose of the car on the ground. Very small front wheels are used, because a large wheel side area would tend to push a top fueler off-course at speed.

FUNNY CARS

Funny cars are very popular with race fans because their fiberglass bodies are based on those found on production automobiles. (Sponsors like them because the bodies provide a lot of space for logos and advertising messages.) They resemble street cars about as much as cartoon characters resemble real humans. They got their name because they looked "funny" to veteran drag racers when they first appeared in the mid-1960s, but there is nothing funny about their abilities. Underneath the skin lies your basic, nitro-burning, top fuel dragster, only with a shorter wheelbase and with the engine sitting in front of the driver.

Funny cars run the quarter mile about a tenth of a second—or 10 miles per hour—slower than top fuel dragsters. Because engine explosions are a fact of life in drag racing, funny cars are equipped with on-board fire extinguishers and roof escape hatches, and some have systems that blow the body off the car should a fire threaten to trap a driver. All drivers wear fire-resistant overalls, gloves, boots, and face masks.

Funny cars also have the multiple-disk clutches, on-board computer data-gathering equipment, and double-parachute brake systems found in top fuel dragsters, and share with them the need to have the engines completely rebuilt, if not replaced, between each round of competition.

PRO STOCK

Pro stock racing is the third major category of professional drag racing. "Stock" simply refers to the fact that the cars' bodies appear to be close matches for the Oldsmobiles, Chevrolets, Pontiacs, Dodges, and Fords found in America's garages and driveways, but that is where the resemblance ends. Pro stock dragsters are pure race cars, built from scratch with carbon-fiber bodies, alloy tube frames, and 500-cubic inch, 1,000-horsepower engines that are fitted with a huge pair of carburetors. They do run on gasoline, but this gasoline has a super high octane rating and cannot be found at any gas station.

Pro stock cars have earned the nickname "doorslammers" from drag racers because, unlike funny cars, they have doors that actually work. Drivers sit in a protective roll cage, needed in cars that reach nearly 200 m.p.h. after a seven-second blast down the quarter mile.

Drivers of pro stock cars, unlike their colleagues in the top fuelers and funny cars, actu-

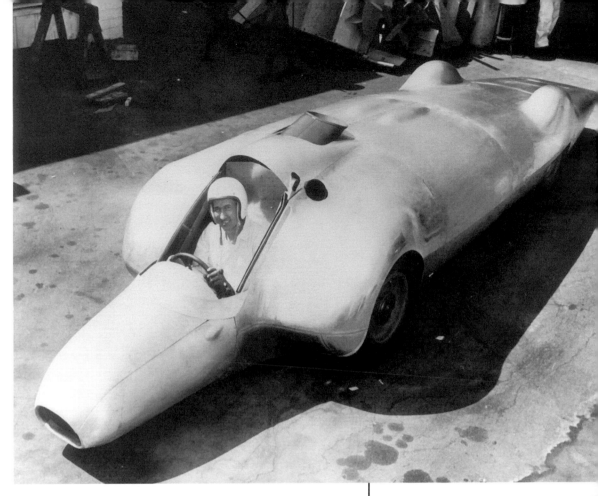

ally have to shift gears during their runs. They keep their eyes on a tachometer which measures engine speed, telling them when to shift. Many use a five-speed transmission, controlled by a push-button system.

Art Arfons used equipment from jet airplanes to make his "Green Monster."

SOMETHING FOR EVERYBODY

Although big-buck top fuelers, funny cars, and pro stock machines make most of drag racing's headlines, drag racing today is actually dominated by amateurs. These speed lovers run in

In 1953, Race queen Bonnie Wallace presented Joaquin Arnett with a trophy after Arnett and his "Bean Bandit" had the fastest race time of the day.

drag racing's many less-expensive classes, which even accommodate street-legal cars that are driven to competitions.

Drag strips are found in every state of the union, as are drag racers who desire nothing more than the satisfaction of winning and the pride of taking a trophy home to place on the mantle. Many race teams are family affairs, with the spouse acting as crew chief and the kids helping to maintain and clean the cars. Indeed, many of today's top drag racing stars, such as Shelly Anderson, grew up in the sport, working on their dad's cars.

The National Hot Rod Association even has started a special competition class for kids, using half-size "top fuelers" that are powered by lawn-mower engines. Reaching a top speed of 30 m.p.h. over a one-eighth mile run, many boys and girls are in this way fueling their dreams of future stardom, with mom and dad cheering them on.

Although the technology has changed over the years, drag racing, in terms of grass-roots appeal, is very much the same sport it was in its infancy. Then, as now, it boils down to two people going head-to-head, trying to prove that each has the faster car.

QUARTER-MILEPOSTS

Drag racing officially began on a two-lane road north of Santa Barbara, California, back in April

1949. A group of local street-racing enthusiasts had arranged a match race between two noted drivers, Fran Hernandez and Tom Cobbs. Hernandez raced a 1932 Ford coupe with no fenders, fitted with a brand-new Mercury V-8, three Stromberg carburetors, and a "trick" manifold. Cobbs had a 1929 Model A Ford roadster, sitting on a 1934 Ford frame, powered by a 1934 Ford V-8 that had a supercharger on top, taken from a diesel truck engine.

Hernandez's car had to be push-started to fire up, and once it did, its fumes told any nose in the know that the coupe had some nitro in its system. A starter waved a white flag, and the cars were off with a roar, Hernandez in front. Cobbs was making up ground at the end of the three-tenths of a mile run, but Hernandez won by a length.

What made this run special was that the organizers, for the first time, had obtained the blessing of the California Highway Patrol to stage the race. Other events soon followed, crowds started to materialize, and before a year had passed, the first organized drag meet, where the audience was charged admission, took place at an abandoned airstrip in Santa Ana, California.

The organizer of the Santa Ana Drags was an Ohio native and former moonshiner named C. J. Hart. He had been a hot-rodder who owned a Model T roadster that his wife, Peggy, drove in competitions. Hart soon replaced his stopwatches with an electronic timing device mounted in an old hearse, which he had the habit of parking about a quarter-mile away from the starting line.

After World War II, hot-rodding became quite popular and was in need of some organization.

There were a lot of unmarried ex-GIs after the war, with plenty of spare bucks and mechanical aptitude honed by the war. Southern California, with all of its know-how invested in wartime aircraft factories, provided ready technical support for guys wanting to soup up an old car. Many of these early hot-rodders were reckless, and the newspapers played up an image of lawlessness as these early racers risked lives breaking the speed limit on public roads.

The public outcry meant that the police would soon issue tickets for "engaging in a speed contest," which carried a heavy fine. Hart was one of the first people to realize that hot-rodders would appreciate a way to take part in their sport without having to worry about the law.

Many hot-rodders took to the wide open spaces of the desert, or the Bonneville Salt Flats in Utah, where horsepower and streamlining allowed their "lakes" machines to achieve unheard-of speeds. Those who remained in relatively confined urban and suburban areas, meanwhile, developed an appreciation for machines that could simply get from Point A to Point B in the shortest amount of time. These racers often stripped their cars of bodies altogether, creating cheap, lightweight "rail" jobs that were the direct ancestors of today's dragsters.

Both groups flocked to the numerous drag strips that were sprouting up all over southern California by 1951. That was also the year that Wally Parks, the editor of *Hot Rod* magazine, founded the National Hot Rod Association. The NHRA was staging races within two years, and Parks used the pages of his magazine to promote the NHRA as a leader for the sport. It was a successful effort. Rival organizations would

Lefty Mudersbach pilots the Chet Herbert twin-engine dragster in 1962.

come and go over the years, but today the NHRA still reigns as the primary sanctioning organization for drag racing.

There was a minimum of regulations in drag racing's early days, but a seemingly infinite number of ideas on how one could get from Point A to Point B first. Such experimentation led to some wild-and-woolly-looking race cars. Engines were mounted front or rear, straight or sideways, low or high, in an effort to transfer weight to the all-important, traction-producing, rear wheels. Multiple engines were used. The Arfons brothers, Art and Walt, of Akron, Ohio, were famous for using gigantic used aircraft engines in their "Green Monster" racers, an approach that would always get them the top speed at drag races, although never the lowest ET.

Parts for cars usually came from junkyards, but one of the early California racers, Joaquin Arnett, hit upon the idea of creating a machine by hand, with a formed steel tube frame and a hand-formed body. The tiny, strong, light machine that resulted, the "Bean Bandit," won many trophies in the early 1950s, and was the first car to use the fabrication techniques found in today's cars.

NHRA's first meet took place in Pomona, California, on a weekend in April 1953. Two thousand spectators showed up on Saturday, and 15,000 on Sunday, and they saw Arnett's new dragster take the trophy for fastest ET at 11.08 seconds.

Records fell over the years as hot-rodders found new secrets of speed. Lloyd Scott's "Bustle Bomb," with its Olds/Cadillac engine, was the first dragster to top 150 m.p.h. when it hit 151 during a run at Great Bend, Kansas, in 1955, as well as the first dragster to record an ET under 10 seconds (9.44), which it did at a meet in San Fernando, California, later that year.

Don Garlits's speed of 176.40 m.p.h., posted in Brooksville, Florida, in 1957, was the first to top 170, as well as the first ET under 9 seconds (8.79). He hit 180 the following year, the last time a nonsupercharged engine set a record, and in 1961 Garlits brought the ET record under eight seconds with a 7.88-second run in Columbia, South Carolina.

In 1964, Garlits's run in Atco, New Jersey, bested the 200-m.p.h. mark for the first time at 201.34. Tommy Allen topped 210 two years later with a 213.76 in Carlsbad, California, and only a year after that, in 1967, the 220 barrier fell with John Edmunds's 226.12 run, also in Carlsbad. That was the year John Mulligan posted the first sub-seven-second ET with a 6.98-second blast in Pomona.

Competitors were starting to strain at the limits of technology in the late 1960s, and records started to take longer to reach. The 230-m.p.h.

mark did not fall until Larry Hendrickson's 232.55 run in Vancouver, B.C., in 1971. Danny Ongais broke 240 the following year with a 243.34 blitz in Ontario, California. A year later, Mike Snively broke the six-second barrier with a 5.97-second ET at Ontario, a record that stood for only a few minutes until Don Moody immediately lowered it to 5.91.

Garlits was the first to top 250 in a top fueler, with a 250.69 speed posted at Ontario in 1975. The 5.63-second ET record he set on the same run was a mark that stood for seven years, until Gary Beck topped it with a 5.54 at Indianapolis Raceway Park.

The sport's current assault on records got under way in the early 1980s when multiple-plate clutches replaced transmissions in top fuelers. Joe Amato's 264.70 m.p.h. posted at Englishtown, New Jersey, in 1984 was the first run over 260; 2 years later Garlits was the first man over 270 with a 272.56-m.p.h. run in Swamp Rat 30, in Gainesville, Florida.

By 1988, Gene Snow had run the first sub-five-second ET, a 4.99 run that electrified the crowd witnessing the feat in Dallas. Connie Kalitta bested 290 with a 291.54 run in Pomona in 1989, and the magical 300-m.p.h. barrier fell when Kenny Bernstein ran a 301.70 in Gainesville on March 20, 1992.

2

BIG DADDY

Don "Big Daddy" Garlits was, during his heyday, the most recognized figure in drag racing. His "Swamp Rat" dragsters consistently set the standard for performance for more than three decades, breaking speed records several times along the way.

But Garlits, a Florida resident, was always perceived as a bit of an outsider by the Californians who largely controlled the sport, and he butted heads with track promoters and the National Hot Rod Association on more than one occasion. Still, Garlits was universally respected for his competitive fire, and for the numerous technological innovations he brought to the sport.

Garlits was born in 1932, the son of a Westinghouse engineer. Don and his younger brother, Ed, earned pocket change repairing bicycles. By the time Don was a high school senior, he had bought his first car, a 1940 Ford sedan, and

Don Garlits poses with his original "Swamp Rat" in 1956. On his left is his wife, Pat, and his brother Ed. On his right is Bob Phillips, out of whose brother's Chrysler the engine had been taken.

was taking metal shop courses in school.

Garlits started his competitive life with street racing in Tampa and St. Petersburg, Florida. His first run in organized competition came when he and his new wife, Pat, entered their 1950 Ford on a whim while visiting the drag strip in Lake Wales, Florida. Don won a trophy that Sunday, and he soon acquired a 1927 Model T Ford roadster that, after he fixed it up as a slingshot dragster, won NHRA's Florida Safari in 1955.

By 1956, Garlits had sold the Ford and created a new slingshot on a narrowed 1930 Chevy frame, powered by a 331-cubic-inch Chrysler hemi-head engine he borrowed from a friend. This, the first "Swamp Rat," was the fastest car in Florida, and it inspired Garlits to think about racing full-time as a career. Track promoters started to offer him money just for showing up and speed manufacturers provided money when he used their equipment.

Garlits, practicing frugality and staying focused, was the first true professional drag racer. He and his young family crisscrossed the country, in search of big races and paydays. A Texas promoter noted Garlits's habit of traveling with his children and gave him the nickname "Daddy," which soon became "Big Daddy" as his reputation grew.

Don opened a performance tuning garage in Tampa to help finance his new career and started to develop a reputation that reached the West Coast. Californians tended to dismiss Garlits as a guy who would compete against questionable clocks with equally dubious equipment, but they were curious about his accomplishments, and few doubted his capacity for innovation, or his bravery.

His first major drag racing accident occurred in 1959, when the supercharger on Swamp Rat 1 exploded in his face. Not entirely aware of what had happened and still feeling his competitive juices, Garlits kept his foot on the gas, causing flames to jet into his face and hands like a blowtorch. (He was wearing a new leather jacket that Pat had given him, which probably saved his life. Garlits in those days normally raced just wearing a T-shirt.) Badly burned, Garlits discovered that the first doctor treating him wanted to amputate one of his hands. A second doctor, who had treated soldiers in Korea who had been badly burned in tanks, soaked his hands in saline for five weeks, which allowed the skin to grow back.

"Swamp Rat III" warms up before a race.

He also narrowly escaped death on the track 11 years later, when a transmission exploded like a hand grenade in Swamp Rat 13 just as he charged off the line. The fragments sliced the rear axle and driver's cage of the slingshot completely off, and the assembly tumbled down the strip with Garlits strapped inside. Mickey Thompson pulled him from the wreckage and noted that the front half of Don's right foot was barely attached. The injury got no help from the ambulance attendant, who managed to slam the ambulance door on the foot. While recovering from this injury, Garlits committed himself to

When Garlits's transmission exploded (a piece of it, circled, can be seen by the rear tire), Garlits and his rollcage were pitched completely loose from the rest of the chassis. Garlits was severely injured in the 1970 accident but later returned with a safer design for a dragster.

creating a rear-engined dragster that would keep flames and exploding components behind the driver when things went wrong.

Garlits suffered other injuries as well. Once, while he was working in a Houston parking lot on his truck, the jack slipped, and the truck fell on his head, giving him a concussion. He sustained a broken back one time when his dragster's parachute failed to open, causing the car to hurtle off the end of the strip, into some trees, and onto a railroad track. Another time, his chute worked too well, stopping the car so suddenly that Garlits's bladder ruptured as his body slammed into his seat belts. This later led to a case of uremic poisoning.

Ed Garlits saved Don from drowning early in his career after an axle snapped on their tow truck while they were returning to Florida from a race, throwing the truck into a canal. On another trip, Don and Pat escaped serious injury when their rig was run over from behind by a drunk driver.

Although it had nearly killed him, Swamp Rat 1 was Garlits's first record-setting dragster, posting a mark of 176.4 m.p.h. in 1957. It also bore evidence of Garlits's genius, as its secret for speed lay in extraordinarily fat fuel lines that were hidden from the prying eyes of competitors in the car's frame rails. More fuel obviously meant more horsepower, and in the loosely-regulated world of drag racing's early days, if you could get away with something, it was legal.

Another notable Garlits machine was Swamp Rat 6, which had "zoom" exhaust headers, pipes that directed exhaust over the tops of the rear slicks. This improved airflow, helped clean bits of rubber off the tires' racing surfaces, and allowed Garlits to break the 200-m.p.h. mark in 1964.

By now, Garlits was wearing a special driving suit that he had developed to protect him from flames. Made of an aluminized fabric, the suit, which soon became standard issue in the sport, caused the wearer to look as though he were an astronaut.

It was Swamp Rat 14 that truly revolutionized the sport of drag racing. This was the car that Garlits designed from his hospital bed in 1971, the car that made the sport safe by locating the engine in the rear. Swamp Rat 22, made four years later, was the vehicle that took Garlits through the 250-m.p.h. mark in 1975 with a 250.69 run. The 5.63-second elapsed time on the run was a record that stood for 17 years.

With Swamp Rat 30, Garlits truly reached the outer boundaries of dragster design. Nearly 28 feet long, it had a Lexan canopy covering the cockpit and a pair of tiny 13-inch wheels in front covered with a fairing. Instead of tires, the front wheels were fitted with skinny Kevlar industrial fan belts.

The small but slippery front end was Swamp Rat 30's speed secret, Garlits claimed. The machine debuted in March 1986 at the NHRA Gatornationals in Gainesville, Florida. The car had a small problem, even though it did well in qualifying and in the early rounds of eliminations: the Kevlar belts kept flying off the front wheels by the time Swamp Rat 30 hit the timing lights at the end of each run. Still, in the semifinals, facing ex-NFL quarterback Dan Pastorini in his "Quarterback Sneak," Garlits broke the 270-m.p.h. mark for the first time, with a 5.409-second ET at 272.56 m.p.h. Thirty years into his competitive career, Garlits had set another record, and the crowd at Gainesville went nuts cheering.

Garlits soon realized that the canopy, though attention-getting (it had a decal on it reading "Rat Under Glass"), weighed too much for the minor improvement in air drag it generated, so he removed it. With the car fitted with conventional front tires, he lowered his E.T. mark to 5.343 seconds in July, qualifying for the NHRA Summernationals at Englishtown, New Jersey.

In eliminations the next day, Garlits was involved in one of drag racing's scariest moments. As he came off the line, the front wheels lifted into the air a little bit, a frequent occurrence in drag racing. As the car was going straight, Garlits kept his foot on the gas, but the wheels kept rising in the air to about a 30-degree angle, at which point the car simply took off at nearly 200 m.p.h.

The car came back down, first on the rear wing, and then on one of the rear tires. The car performed a snap pivot and crashed to the track still moving along at high speed, but pointed backwards.

Garlits, disoriented from the smoke, still had his foot on the gas. The car traveled 100 yards backward as Garlits inadvertently performed a giant burnout, slowed to a brief stop, and then started charging back toward the starting line!

As the car roared out of the smoke, the course workers scattered in all directions as Swamp Rat 30 barreled along. Finally Garlits realized what was going on and managed to brake the dragster to a stop. Mesmerized, the crowd watched Garlits climb out of the cockpit, unscathed, and then throw his hands up in the air, elated at having beat out the Grim Reaper once again.

Garlits would go on to win the top fuel championship again that year. He claimed it was due to the aerodynamic efficiency of Swamp Rat 30's front fairing, but Garlits was known to be a sneaky competitor. Garlits had relocated and hidden the car's fuel tank under the fairing ahead of the front axle, dramatically transferring the dragster's weight distribution forward to help keep the front wheels on the ground. This allowed Garlits to transfer more power to the ground with the use of a tighter clutch and a lower gear.

But the following year found Garlits's spirit considerably frustrated as the top fuel field had grown closely competitive. Swamp Rat 30 missed qualifying for several races, and it was August 1987 before its successor, Swamp Rat 31, made its debut. At its second appearance in Spokane, Washington, the car flipped, Garlits's third major wreck in as many years. As was the case in the previous year, a rear wing that was either too large or too far back had caused the dragster to pivot up on its rear axle and wreck. Garlits was unhurt, but he had had enough, and retired for two years.

In 1989, Garlits borrowed Shirley Muldowney's top fueler and ran some races. In 1992, he rolled out Swamp Rat 32 in an attempt to be the first driver to break 300 m.p.h., but he suffered a detached retina after pulling the parachutes in a practice run, and finally retired for good.

Today, Garlits spends his time as a consultant to other race teams, doing color commentary for television broadcasts, and tending to the Big Daddy Don Garlits Museum of Drag Racing, just off I-75 in Ocala, Florida, adjacent to his home.

During his career, Garlits was known to be a rebel. The NHRA had put a temporary ban on fuel competition in the late 1950s and early 1960s, which Garlits, a nitro proponent, believed was a means of keeping him out of competition. He had made a few good gasoline runs that winter, and one day he, brother Ed, and longtime friend Art Malone went to the Spruce Creek, Florida, strip to run an NHRA meet. Garlits made his way into the final round, competing against Alabama's Lewis Carden. The flagman waved, Garlits took off, but Carden exercised his option not to take the start. Seeing what happened, Garlits slowed down, turned around and drove back up the strip. While Garlits and Malone were getting the dragster positioned for its normal push-start, NHRA head Wally Parks walked over and told Garlits he was through for the evening, disqualified for crossing the center line when he turned his dragster around, and that Carden was going to make a solo run for the win.

Garlits works on preparing his car for a 1982 race with nephew Ed Garlits Jr.

His temper flaring, Garlits waved for Malone to push him forward in the truck. Parks chose that moment to step between the rear of the dragster and the push car, just as Malone started to accelerate. Parks made a wild leap onto the hood of the push car as Garlits took off down the asphalt, catching Carden at midstrip. But even as he completed his run, Garlits figured he had competed in his last NHRA contest for awhile.

His feuds with Parks would continue over the years, but the sanctioning body quickly forgave Garlits, particularly after it reinstated fuel competition. Parks simply had to acknowledge that Don Garlits was the biggest star in drag racing, and its most innovative competitor. The sport would never have reached the heights of popularity it enjoys today without Garlits's exploits captivating fans, and this fact remains Big Daddy's lasting legacy.

THE SNAKE

Back in the 1950s, when Dwight D. Eisenhower was the U.S. president and television was starting to take hold of the American public, a young Californian named Don Prudhomme started to get interested in drag racing.

His dad was a Texan and his mom was from Louisiana. His parents had lived in Los Angeles since the 1930s, and after a while they had moved to Van Nuys. Young Don's interest in cars was fueled as he hung around his dad's body shop, and as he grew up he earned pocket money painting cars.

His first car was a 1948 Mercury which he soon sold to get a 1950 Olds Rocket 88. He raced along streets among the orange groves of the San Fernando Valley, and, hooked, started to experiment with bigger and better hardware.

By the early 1960s, he was taking his cars to the tracks, and in 1962 he won what was at the time the premier race for fuelers, the Smokers

Don Prudhomme behind the wheel of a top fueler.

Meet at Bakersfield, California, driving a 1927 Model T powered by a supercharged 392-cubic-inch Chrysler. His driving talent was immediately obvious, and young Don started to dream of becoming a professional racer.

Prudhomme hooked up with noted engine man Keith Black and chassis specialist Kent Fuller and the trio started racing California fuel meets in 1962. They learned to match horsepower to whatever each track they raced would take. Over the two-and-a-half years the team was together, Prudhomme won about nine out of 10 races against the likes of Garlits and "TV" Tommy Ivo (one of the original "Mouseketeers" from television's early days). The team charged $1,000 to make an appearance and grossed $22,000 the first year alone—an unheard-of sum in those days.

The team also had the know-how to stay in front with technology. Drag racers have always faced a choice in terms of coping with the unbelievable amounts of horsepower at their disposal: either overpower the strip and spin the tires, or reduce power and wheelspin and cause a wheelstand (or "wheelie"). Managing this balance required a careful matchup of chassis and engine. Garlits was an advocate of the spin-the-tires-in-a-cloud-of-smoke school; Black felt the key to performance was to minimize wheelspin but allow controlled slippage of engine output through the clutch.

Black's clutch tinkering paid off on January 20, 1963, with a run Prudhomme made at San Gabriel, California. After the flag fell, witnesses felt the run would be no good, because there was hardly any detectable smoke coming off the tires at all. In fact, Prudhomme had set a new national elapsed time record of 7.77 seconds, about three-tenths of a second faster than what the best fuelers of the day were running.

Prudhomme won the very first NHRA race he ever entered, the 1965 Winternationals, driving a top fuel slingshot dragster owned by Roland Leong, known as "The Hawaiian." When he won the U.S. Nationals later that same year, he became the first driver to win the two major events in the same year.

During the course of his spectacular driving career, Prudhomme won 49 NHRA races—14 in top fuel, and 35 driving funny cars. He was the first driver to win four straight funny car championships (1975-1978). Those 49 wins came in 68 finals, a winning total second only to that of pro stock's Bob Glidden (see next chapter). Prudhomme was 35 for 45 in funny car finals, 14 for 23 in top fuel competition. Over his career, Prudhomme won 389 of the 589 elimination rounds he faced, for a .660 winning percentage.

In his prime, Prudhomme was a deadlock cinch to win, particularly in funny cars. He won seven of eight series races in 1976, part of a 13-for-16 stretch between 1975 and 1976.

He was the first funny car pilot to run under six seconds, which he did with a 5.98-second run in 1975. He was also the first to break the 5.7-second barrier with a 5.63 run in 1982; the first under 5.2 (5.193 seconds, 1989); and the first funny car driver to break the 250-m.p.h. speed barrier, with a 250.00-flat run in 1982.

No slouch as a top fuel pilot, he was the third dragster pilot to exceed 300 m.p.h., with a 301.60 m.p.h. in 1993.

Prudhomme drove dragsters until 1973, when he switched to the stock-bodied funny cars, and

Don Prudhomme and top rival Tom McEwen pose for a race promotion.

then he returned to top fuel competition in 1990. Always a showman, Prudhomme realized early on that the relatively expansive sheet metal offered by funny cars made them an attractive proposition to sponsors, as well as something that fans could easily relate to. They simply looked more like what was parked in the family driveway than Garlits's Swamp Rats did.

In those early days, the NHRA saw the funny cars primarily as a form of entertainment to fill out available time during a race weekend. "We were living race to race and barnstorming the country," Prudhomme says of those early funny car days. "We were basically a circus act. We'd go in and set up and perform, and pack up and leave. Those were the years we were really fighting for survival."

When drag racing received major serieswide corporate sponsorship in 1975, funny car racing was fully legitimized as class competition, and Prudhomme's career took off. Nobody could touch The Snake as he mowed down all comers while taking the funny car titles in 1975 and 1976. His sole defeats in 1975 came at Englishtown and Indianapolis; he only lost once in 1976, at the Nationals at Indy.

As his driving career wound down, he became subject to the incredibly tight competition that marked top fuelers, and some frustration set in. Prudhomme endured the longest losing streak of his career, a 27-race stretch that dated back to 1992, before he stopped the bleeding with a win at Houston in 1994, during his final year of competition. When the win finally came, The Snake was ecstatic. "I've had some great thrills over the years, but this was special," Prudhomme said of his Houston win. "I knew I was in the groove as a driver, but these days, being there has a lot to do with the people around you," a reference to his crew and crew chief Wes Cerny. "I owe that one to Wes. He turned things around for me and gave me the confidence a driver has to have."

In 1994, Prudhomme, by then 54 years of age, finally quit drag racing as a driver. His exit was auspicious. Running in top fuel competition, Prudhomme won three NHRA races his final year, finished second twice, won the Winston Invitational all-star meet and wound up second in the points to Scott Kalitta.

That final year was an emotional one for Prud-homme. Dubbed "The Snake" in the 1960s because of his lightning-quick reaction times, Prudhomme, in his "Final Strike" tour, enjoyed tribute from thousands of fans who came out just to say good-bye. Some fans recalled him from his early top-fuel days when he drove front-engined dragsters and won five national events. Many recalled his pioneering campaigns in fun-ny cars when he and fellow racer Tom McEwen were popularized by Mattel Toys' "Snake and Mongoose" Hot Wheels sets.

Respect was an important component in Prud-homme's final year as a competitor. "I just like to be respected at the race tracks," he said. "When I walked back to the pits, the racers tipped their caps to me a little bit. As long as they respect me as being a tough guy to beat, that's good enough. I like that."

When asked to describe his legacy as a race driver, Prudhomme replied, "Success and longevity. I hope that the fans and drivers see me as a pretty good racer. I don't think I was ever the best out there," he said modestly. "I felt I was pretty tough to beat, though. To be able to stay in the sport as long as I did and be com-petitive for 30 years, that's something. Some guys are competitive for a year or two. Try 30!"

But even in his heyday as a driver, Prud-homme was notable for exhibiting a fundamen-tal amount of common sense in approaching drag racing as a business. Don Garlits had paved the way for drivers making a living, albeit a tough one, as drag racers. Prudhomme, in turn, was among the first to find ways to make a drag rac-ing career commercially viable by exploiting

Don Prudhomme is off to another fast start in his famous "Snake" funny car.

sponsorships, particularly from companies not directly linked to the automotive industry, and reducing his personal financial risk to a minimum.

Starting in 1967, Prudhomme signed on to drive a top fueler owned by Lou Baney. The car was powered by a Ford engine from the shop of noted engine builder Ed Pink, and sponsored by the legendary Carroll Shelby, the father of the Ford Cobra sportscar and a mainstay of Ford Motorsports. In the past, Prudhomme admitted to being totally ignorant of race car technology, preferring to concentrate on developing his skills as a driver. This time he absorbed everything, ultimately developing decent mechanical and management skills, and after two years he felt he was ready to start running his own car.

"The Snake" had developed a reputation as one of the top drivers in the sport, and soon an old friend and rival, Tom McEwen, started campaigning under the nickname of "The Mongoose," as the animal was one of the few creatures that was able to take on a snake. McEwen had relatives working at Mattel Toy Company, and sent them a sponsorship proposal on behalf of "Wildlife Racing Enterprises"—The Snake and The Mongoose. The next thing Prudhomme and McEwen knew, they were racing two top fuelers and two funny cars under the biggest sponsorship budget the sport had ever known. Other marketers were impressed by the duo, and threw their money into the team as well: Coca-Cola, Plymouth, Goodyear, and Wynn's (an automotive lubricants company) all contributed.

The pair did very well, competing in several match races a week during racing season (with McEwen being loudly booed by crowds as the bad guy), making endorsements, doing interviews, creating a television special. The deal lasted three years, and Prudhomme managed to gross about $400,000 in 1972, primarily from offshoot activities associated with the sponsorship, with less than $50,000 of that coming from winnings in actual open competition.

After the Mattel deal expired, Prudhomme was able to continue competing under sponsorship from companies such as Wendy's, Pepsi-Cola, Plymouth, and even the U.S. Army. Having all of this financial backing did nothing to soften his competitive drive, however. He won the NHRA Nationals two years in a row, a feat that previously had only been achieved by Garlits.

With a career spanning more than three decades, Prudhomme has a wide perspective on just how far drag racing safety has come. During his first NHRA victory in 1965, Prudhomme's top fuel slingshot clocked a 7.76-second run at 201.34 m.p.h. His best run towards the end of his career was 302.72 m.p.h. in 1990. "I'd rather run 300 in today's cars than 200 back in the '60s," Prudhomme allows. "It's so much safer today, especially with the race tracks. You'd be shocked at the lack of safety facilities 30 years ago. It wasn't that people were skimping on safety, it was just that nobody knew any different."

Nowadays, Prudhomme owns the Miller Racing top fuel team, with Larry Dixon, NHRA's 1995 Rookie of the Year, as driver. As a team owner, Prudhomme has finally become a fully rounded drag racing competitor, not merely one of the sport's hottest drivers.

4

BOB GLIDDEN

Chances are, if you've ever seen a picture of Bob Glidden, he's probably holding a trophy over his head. There are two reasons for this: (1) he tends to be somewhat shy, and is not the sort of guy who'll grandstand for the camera just for the heck of it, and (2) he's held a lot of trophies over his head, creating a lot of photo opportunities for those shooters covering drag racing.

This last point is true because nobody in the sport has won more trophies than Bob Glidden. The man has won an incredible 85 NHRA national pro stock events, and he's won the pro stock world championship 10 times.

Glidden is drag racing personified. The 1996 season marked his 25th year in the sport, and he was closing in on making his 300th career start.

A native of Whiteland, Indianapolis, Glidden holds many national records, including most

Bob Glidden has won more races than any other driver.

consecutive wins (9), most consecutive times as number one qualifier (23), and more elimination victories and final-round appearances than anyone in the history of the NHRA.

Glidden attributes his success to running a close-knit, family race team. Etta, his wife, is his crew chief, and is acknowledged by competitors to be one of the best there is, and Glidden claims that she has been integral to his success. His sons Rusty and Bill grew up around racing, have served as crew members for their dad, and have both gone on to be pro stock competitors, with Bill currently serving as his dad's teammate, driving for Ford Quality Care.

Competitors have acknowledged that one advantage Glidden has in running a family team is that blood ties enhance security. He has always been an enormously secretive person, and has publicly stated that unless your last name is Glidden, you have no business looking at his engine parts.

His achievements gained Glidden induction into the Motorsports Hall of Fame in 1994. His tenacity can be seen in the fact that his 85th win, at the 1995 NHRA Nationals in Englishtown, came after a two-year dry spell. Prior to his winless 1994, he had managed to win at least one national event in each of his 23 seasons drag racing. His success has put him at the top echelons of the sport, and he is one of the few people (Garlits, Prudhomme, and funny-car ace John Force are others) to have become wealthy through drag racing.

The only national event Glidden did not attempt to qualify for was the 1995 NHRA Winternationals, because he had suffered a heart attack in December 1994 and was recovering from a six-way coronary bypass operation. His son Rusty took over driving duties until the 1995 Phoenix event, when Glidden stepped back into the cockpit, a mere seven weeks after surgery.

Glidden has dominated pro stock competition his entire career. Of his 10 championships, five (from 1985 through 1989) were consecutive. Glidden had qualified for an incredible 107 consecutive NHRA events until mechanical problems sidelined him one day in 1990. A victory in the Winston Finals, the last event of the year, clinched Glidden a second-place finish in the standings that year.

The man is a natural mechanic. He first turned wrenches fixing the family tractor at the age of 14, and he once held a job as a line mechanic at an Indiana Ford dealership. He learned the value of good preparation early in life, and his competitors will say that there is nobody in drag racing who has a more dedicated work ethic than Bob Glidden.

Glidden insists on doing a lot of his own work, and is almost always tinkering with the car when he is not actually sitting in it. He has always kept his focus on what he does best, which is why he has always competed in pro stock, and why he has almost always raced Fords.

Glidden and his wife started out as weekend hobby racers, staging for trophies in a 1962 Ford. When attractive purses started to become

"Dyno" Don Nicholson has a fireproof suit on as he sits behind the wheel of his funny car.

a reality, the Gliddens decided to try to make a living at racing.

His first race car as a pro was a 1972 Ford Pinto, and Glidden, thanks to his mechanical expertise and willingness to tinker, was tough from the beginning. He was regarded as an expert at preparing intake manifolds and heads, and had a reputation for preparing some of the most powerful engines in pro stock competition.

The career brought with it a lot of work: on the car, driving, securing sponsorships, making public appearances, and shooting commercials for Ford. Even during the brief periods, such as in 1994, when Glidden wasn't winning, he knew he couldn't fault his approach, and figured that, at least for a while, luck had strayed from him.

The times luck was with him, his hard-working approach was what created it. Since Ford started officially sponsoring him in 1983, Glidden has won 23 percent of all NHRA national events and has been in the finals of 32 percent of those events.

He enjoyed a particular hot streak driving Ford Thunderbirds between 1983 and 1988, when he piloted T-Birds to 30 wins, winning 39 percent of all NHRA national events during that time. He started driving a Ford Probe in 1988, and that first Probe won nine of 19 events in 1989.

Glidden, thanks to his preparation, has always been known as a reliable qualifier; since 1983 he has qualified number one 44 times out of 181 national events.

He has finished in the top 10 of the pro stock championship points standings for 22 consecutive years, from 1974 to 1995; as of July 1996 Glidden had a career record of 783 wins against 208 losses, nearly an 80-percent success rate.

His level of preparation for drag races is such that he has often beat the competition even before showing up for an event. With hard work and solid preparation, Glidden believes that success will come with enough decent runs and knowing to do the best job possible when you've got an advantage.

Perhaps no meet better illustrates this point than the final event on the 1980 calendar, which took place at Ontario Speedway in California. Glidden went into this last race in second place in the points, behind Lee Shepherd, who seemed to have a lock on the championship. An incredible combination of circumstances would have to occur for Shepherd to lose the title: he'd have to be eliminated in the second round, Glidden would have to win the meet, as well as set the top speed and low ET for the weekend as well. Shepherd did indeed get eliminated in the second round, and, while running to victory in the final, Glidden did indeed set the top speed and low elapsed time for the meet. The 1980 champion: Bob Glidden.

In the opinion of many, running a pro stock car competitively with any consistency is about the most difficult feat in professional drag racing. Top fuelers and funny cars, with 6,000-horsepower, supercharged, nitro-burning engines, are less sensitive to atmospheric conditions than normally aspirated pro stock machines, and, with five times the power, can often rely on sheer brute force to win events. Pro stock drivers also have the added challenge of having to run through a five-speed transmission during the course of a seven-second pass through the quarter mile.

For all this, pro stock racing is extraordinar-

Bob Glidden does a wheelie in his Ford Thunderbird as he moves up to the starting line of the 1984 NHRA Summer Nationals. Glidden earned his 40th career win with a speed of 178.21 mph.

ily popular with fans, and many credit the class with saving the sport as a whole. Many competitors in the late 1960s were unhappy about how stock cars were evolving into expensive funny cars, while others were turned off by the sheer expense, and danger, associated with running nitromethane fuel. Major sponsorships were hard to find, the Vietnam War was reducing attendance figures at meets, and operating expenses were getting out of hand for racers who often traveled more than 50,000 miles a year just to compete.

By 1969, several competitors, including Bill "Grumpy" Jenkins, Don Nicholson, and the team of Ronnie Sox and Buddy Martin put together a set of rules for a class that called for stock-bodied cars to run on stock chassis, powered by gas-burning engines. The idea was a hit from the start, particularly with the major Detroit auto makers. The NHRA saw the class as a means of infusing financial support to competitors, and some political maneuvering on the part of the sanctioning body helped ensure that Ford, General Motors, and Chrysler would all stay interested.

Chrysler cars, such as Sox and Martin's Plymouth, or Dick Landy's Dodge, dominated pro stock's early days, because their Chrysler engines had powerful hemispherical combustion heads, as compared to the conventional "wedge" heads found in Ford or Chevrolet engines. The NHRA soon allowed Fords and Chevys to run at a lighter weight than the Chrysler cars, to help keep things competitive.

Grumpy Jenkins, driving a Chevrolet, immediately realized he could take advantage of this fact, and had a fabricator create a lightweight tubular-frame chassis for a 1972 Chevy Vega body. The car was very successful, winning six major events in 1972, and soon Ford adherents such as Wayne Gapp, Don Nicholson, and ultimately, Bob Glidden, caught on. Pro stock racing had arrived, and soon the stage was set for Mr. Glidden to start his incredible run as the undisputed master of drag racing.

5

A LIFE IN DRAG RACING

By every standard, Shelly Anderson is fully representative of the modern-day drag racer. She has complete knowledge of just what makes her top fuel dragster go. She is a relentless competitor in one of the most competitive divisions in all of motor racing. She is popular with the fans and a knowledgeable and articulate representative for her sponsors.

But more than anything, Shelly Anderson is a winner, as she demonstrated with her May 5, 1996, win at the Pennzoil Nationals in Richmond, Virginia, for her second career victory. She defeated two-time defending top fuel champion Scott Kalitta with a run of 4.779 seconds/298.90 m.p.h. in the finals, as well as five-time champion Joe Amato and points leader Rance McDaniel in eliminations.

Born in 1965, Anderson comes from a drag racing family. Her dad, Brad, won the NHRA's

Shelly Anderson relaxes before a race with crew chief Larry Meyer.

top alcohol funny car championship three times, in 1984, 1985, and 1989. He also owns Brad Anderson Enterprises, a manufacturer of racing engine components, as well as the racing teams of Shelly and her brother, Randy, who won the top alcohol funny car titles in 1993 and 1994.

A native of Denver, Colorado, Shelly grew up in the sport and could totally disassemble and put back together a race car by the time she was a teenager. She spent several years serving as crew chief on her dad's championship team, but ultimately she wanted to drive. Knowing the dangers of the sport, her father insisted that she complete college first, hoping that Shelly might find something else that interested her.

Dad's strategy did not work. She began competing in the top alcohol dragster category after graduating from Cal State/Fullerton in 1991 with a degree in communications, and she had moved up to the top fuel category by the end of the following season.

Since that first season, Anderson has steadily gained in the points standings, finishing at a career-best ninth in 1995. The team, sponsored by Western Auto and Texaco Havoline, is known for its preparation and achieving consistent results in qualifying. Anderson scored her first victory at the season-opening Winternationals in Pomona in 1994, defeating Rance McDaniel. She also won the nonpoints Budweiser Classic at Pomona at the end of that same season.

In this interview, conducted during a rare weekend visit to her home in Upland, California, Shelly Anderson describes the highs and lows of competing at the top echelon of drag racing.

Shelly's team owner is her father, Brad Anderson, a former racing champ himself.

How did your background prepare you to be the driver of a big league top fueler?

I think that by growing up in the sport, I knew what to expect. I didn't go out there starry-eyed—I knew it was a job.

I grew up on the road, and you've got to travel to all the race tracks and stay in a motel—it's not a lot of fun. It's not a party atmosphere—you've got to be serious. When I leave the track at 11:00 p.m. or 12 midnight, I go straight back to the motel and go to bed. There's no partying, and it's all early mornings. So I knew what the life was like, because my dad was serious about the sport. He didn't go to a race to qualify or just contend—he went to win. We knew what it took, and I think that helped.

The early exposure also helped with my development as a driver. I got to see a lot of cars run my entire life—you saw good things and bad things, and you saw when people made mistakes.

What is the most important physical attribute that a drag racer should have?
Good reflexes. You also have to stay calm. If you're going to be scared, you're going to get hurt, and your reflexes aren't going to take over when you get into trouble. I've had a couple of very close calls, and it wasn't anything I did consciously that saved me, it was my reflexes. Once the motor starts, I'm the calmest I ever am.

Do you have a training or conditioning program?
I do aerobics and I also have a gym at home, with a stair machine, an exercise bike, a treadmill, and a lot of other stuff. I also try to eat well. I don't eat fried foods. I eat a lot of vegetables and fruit.

You're obviously a most competitive person.
Absolutely.

Do you ever have to "psych up" before a run?
Nope.

Do you do anything to clear your head to focus?
Yes, I go through the run in my mind over and over, trying to visualize and anticipate anything that might happen, and what I'll do to deal with

it. For example, what happens if you smoke the tires? You pedal it. If the car starts to shake, the tires will break loose if you keep your foot on the throttle. I go through it all.

Can you improve reaction times out of the cockpit with exercises?

Yes, we have a tree, a portable tree, that I use. [The "Christmas Tree" is a sequentially timed series of colored lights used to start drag races. When the final green lamp flashes on, the race is on.]

You must get scares occasionally—how do you manage fear?

I don't get scared. If you get scared, you're going to get hurt. I don't think I have fear. It's a career, it's a business. When we go out there, we know the cars are made to be as safe as possible. If there's any question about it, Dad will handle it.

Safety's number one on everybody's mind at NHRA, as it is with my family and crew, so I really don't worry about it. When we have a close call and something happens, that's when you realize how safe the sport is.

How much of your time is dedicated to fulfilling sponsorship commitments?

It's all the time right now. When you called, I was signing something for Texaco to send back to them. I have a radio interview today between 2:00 and 4:00, for the next race in Kansas City, which is our sponsor's headquarters. This weekend is only my fourth weekend home this year, and it's already July—it's been busy, and it's getting more so every year. And it's not like I only

Shelly Anderson enjoyed her greatest day of racing at the 1996 Winston Select Finals.

race—I come back here and help out with my dad's business. My sister runs the business, and I come back here and help out when I can.

Who were your mentors and heroes in drag racing?

My dad, and Jim Dunn. Dunn still drives an NHRA funny car on the West Coast, and I always watched him run. He and dad were the two drivers I always looked up to.

You got a college degree before you stepped into the cockpit. Why?

My dad said I had to or he wasn't going to let me drive. The sponsor came and said that they wanted to have me drive for them, and dad said as soon as she graduates. And that's fine.

At the time, I didn't like his decision, but now

I do have an education that I can fall back on in case I ever lose my sponsors and I'm not racing, I have something I can do for a career. He was right. I went to school for speech communications, and that has helped with the public appearances that I do. If I didn't have sponsors and wasn't able to race, I'd want to be a newscaster for television.

Did you find you had to work through a series of classes to develop your skills as a driver?
No, I went from driving nothing to driving an alcohol dragster.

That's a big jump.
It was huge. I had never staged a race car until I had staged an alcohol dragster and went 240. From there to nitro wasn't anywhere near as big a jump. The alcohol car was harder to drive, but I really enjoyed it, and I think that because I grew up in the sport I enjoyed it more. I moved up to top fuel competition because my sponsor told me I was going to. You do what your sponsor says.

They wanted that prime-time television exposure.
Yes. Only two months into my driving the alcohol car they signed a deal with dad to move me into a fuel car.

Let's discuss your team. How many chassis and engines do you have at any one time?
I have three chassis, and we always go to a race with six or seven engines.

Are there different setups for different drag

strips? What are the variables?

We do set up in a particular way for each strip, and one of the things we have to allow for is different atmospheric conditions. For example, at Denver, because the air is so thin, we'll go and change the rod length, speed the timing up, and put more blower on. Even the race at Topeka this weekend—it will be so hot, the last 2 years it's been 103 degrees in the shade—so we'll definitely have to put more horsepower into it, we'll run more nitro, change the compression, speed up the timing. There's a lot of things you can do in top fuel competition, unlike in pro stock with a normally aspirated motor, where you're stuck. In nitro competition we can give the car more power.

There is usually a technical breakthrough before speeds go up appreciably in this sport—where might the next one come from?

Well, the latest one has been the electrical magnetos, but the next step should come with clutches. We still have some problems with clutches—some wear, some don't; some work faster than others—there's a long way we can go with clutches.

What does it take day in and day out to be successful in this sport?

A dedicated team. It's a team sport, and you're only as good as your crew. Larry [Larry Meyer, her crew chief] is the type of guy who takes the job home with him and thinks about it all the time. I think that's why our car is doing so well. He's a hands-on crew chief, he doesn't expect any member of the crew to do anything that he wouldn't do, and he can do everything.

How do you feel your competitors view you?

Safe, equal. We all put our helmets on and go race. I've heard one guy say he hates losing to me because I'm a girl, I look at that as an indication that his intelligence level isn't very high. I've never heard that from anybody else.

When I got sponsorship to go racing, I received a lot of calls and cards in the mail congratulating me. And when I moved up to top fuel, all of the fuel drivers came over and congratulated me. There was one that said, "Oh, movin' up to the big boys?," and I said, "No, I'm just changing classes."

Racing's racing. If you want to win, you're going to have to do a lot of work.

You probably get questions from youngsters all the time.

That's the best part about racing—meeting the kids. They're absolutely wonderful, they're honest, and they ask some really good questions. I got a letter last week that's right here in my file cabinet—a girl drew a picture of my race car, and she sent a picture of her and me together— she looks to be about five years old—and she said she was looking forward to seeing me at the next race at Sears Point.

So what do you tell her when, 10 years down the road, she comes up to you again and asks you what you need to do to get involved in drag racing?

Get an education. Go to college. Without an education you're not going to do anything. Drag racing is so hard to depend on, you need something to fall back on. I now understand my father saying—even though the sponsor wanted me—that I had to graduate first. And he was right—I'm glad I did it. It cut several years off my racing, but that's okay, I have an education.

STATISTICS

Top 15 Fastest Speeds in NHRA History

Speed	Driver	Date	Location
314.46	Kenny Bernstein, Dallas	Oct. 30, 1994	Pomona, Calif.
312.50	Joe Amato, Old Forge, Pa.	Oct. 29, 1995	Pomona, Calif.
311.85	Kenny Bernstein	Oct. 30, 1994	Pomona, Calif.
311.52	Larry Dixon, Granada Hills, Calif.	Oct. 29, 1995	Pomona, Calif.
311.31	Kenny Bernstein	March 12, 1995	Baytown, Texas
310.77	Joe Amato	March 12, 1995	Baytown, Texas
310.13	Blaine Johnson, Santa Maria, Calif.	Feb. 17, 1995	Chandler, Ariz.
310.02	Joe Amato	Oct. 15, 1995	Ennis, Texas
309.38	Joe Amato	Oct. 28, 1995	Pomona, Calif.
309.27	Cory McClenathan, Irvine, Calif.	Oct. 28, 1995	Pomona, Calif.
309.17	Kenny Bernstein	May 20, 1995	Englishtown, NJ
309.17	Joe Amato	June 30, 1995	Topeka, Kan.
309.06	Joe Amato	Feb. 17, 1995	Chandler, Ariz.
308.95	Scott Kalitta, Chelsea, Mich.	Sept. 18, 1994	Reading, Pa.
308.95	Cory McClenathan	May 19, 1995	Englishtown, NJ

Source: National Hot Rod Assoc.

CHRONOLOGY

1949   Fran Hernandez wins the first drag race sanctioned by the California Highway Patrol

1951   Wally Parks, editor of *Hot Rod* magazine, founds the National Hot Rod Association

1953   The NHRA holds its first race. Joaquin Arnett's "Bean Bandit"—the first car to use fabrication techniques now used in all dragsters—establishes itself as the car to beat

1955   Lloyd Scott is the first driver to top 150 mph

1957   Don Garlits tops 170 mph for the first time

1958   Don Garlits is the first driver to top 180 mph

1964   Don Garlits is the first driver to top 200 mph. He wears a special driving suit to protect him from flames—a suit he helped design

1965   Don Prudhomme becomes the first driver to win both major championships the same year

1970   Don Garlits is severely injured when Swamp Rat 13's transmission explodes. While recovering, Garlits designed a rear-engined dragster that would be safer—a design that all cars now use

1971   Larry Hendrickson tops 230 mph for the first time

1972   Danny Ongais breaks 240 mph for the first time

1975   Don Garlits is the first driver to top 250 mph

1984   Joe Amato is the first driver to top 260 mph

1986   Don Garlits is the first driver to top 270 mph—over 30 years after he started racing competitively

1989   Connie Kalitta tops 290 for the first time

1992   Kenny Bernstein is the first driver to top 300 mph

SUGGESTIONS FOR FURTHER READING

Garlits, Don, *"Big Daddy": The Autobiography of Don Garlits.* Ocala, FL: Self-published, 1990.

Hawley, Frank, with Mark Smith, *Drag Racing: Drive to Win.* Osceola, WI: Motorbooks International, 1989.

Higdon, Hal. *Six Seconds to Glory: Don Prudhomme's Greatest Drag Race.* New York: G. P. Putnam's Sons, 1975.

Post, Robert C., *High Performance: the Culture and Technology of Drag Racing, 1950-1990.* Baltimore: The Johns Hopkins University Press, 1994.

Sakkis, Tony, *Racing History: Drag Racing Legends.* Osceola, WI: Motorbooks International, 1996.

Sox, Ronnie, and Buddy Martin, *The Sox and Martin Book of Drag Racing.* Washington, DC: Henry Regnery Co., 1974.

ABOUT THE AUTHOR

Paul Cockerham is a journalist who has written for numerous automobile magazines. He lives in New York City.

INDEX

PHOTO CREDITS

Marc Gewertz/NHRA: 2; Hearst Collection, Department of Special Collections, USC Library: 6, 12, 15, 16: Jere Alhadeff Photography: 9, 32, 36, 39, 42, 45; Courtesy National Hot Rod Association: 19, 56; Courtesy Museum of Drag Racing, 22, 25, 26, 31; AP/Wide World Photos: 48; Teresa Long/NHRA: 50; Courtesy Western Auto: 53.